MAEBY & ME

Maeby & Me

RECIPES & STORIES OF HOW ONE HUMAN
& HER DOG DESSERT TOGETHER

JEN AUGELLO

PHOTOGRAPHY BY NICK HOLMES

To Maeby

TABLE OF CONTENTS

INTRODUCTION

After seven years of baking homemade treats for Maeby, we are sharing our story and our favorite dessert recipes with you! This is the first book designed so that you can both make a dog friendly version of your dessert and so you can make a people pleasing version of your dog's treat!

In 2013, I adopted an incredibly sweet puppy who I named Maeby. Our first walk was a funny encounter of us trying to observe each other, but there was an instant connection. Since that day, we've had so many great adventures. Maeby is the sweetest, most adorable companion. She is silly, smart, and tough, but she's very opinionated and knows what she wants. A notorious bacon thief, she's a dairy lover who prefers to sit on the highest and cushiest cushion. And even though balloons really scare her, you can always count on calming her down by lifting her backside up with your foot.

On Maeby's first birthday, I bought her a dog friendly pupcake, but her reaction was pretty anticlimactic. Moving forward, because I am that dog lady, I decided to use my love of baking to spoil Maeby on her birthdays and gotcha days. Each year, I obsessed over what treat I was going to make her. I had two boxes to check: (1) she needed to love it even more than the year before & (2) I wanted it to look beautiful. I started with a list of dog friendly ingredients I knew she loved, and I would brainstorm ideas of what to make her based on human desserts. What used to be an annual brainstorming process started to subconsciously occur while baking for myself throughout the year. It's been a seven-year tradition of baking some seriously special treats that she and I have both enjoyed. And last year, I realized I had enough recipes to write a book, so here we are!

You'll hopefully notice from our photos and the bakes themselves that spending time in the kitchen with your pup is really all about having fun with your furry friend. Maeby spoils me every day with her love and affection, so it's nice every now and again to demonstrate how much she means to me by whipping up some fresh treats just for her.

While some recipes have worked really well, others have been a complete disaster. Though these are all really fun to make, some recipes can be a bit temperamental or require some creativity since I designed them to make smaller batches. Don't worry if you don't have the perfect baking dish or need to slightly adjust the recipe to get the right texture. The best part about baking for your dog? They just want to spend time with you and are grateful for the treat even if it's not perfect.

HOW TO USE THIS BOOK

The recipes in this book are meant to be a special (and occasional) treat for you and your pup. Aside from recipe testing for the release of this book, I typically only make Maeby treats like this once or twice a year - her birthday and Gotcha Day! Maeby is 7 years old, so if you do the math, you'll see that I've been prepping & planning for her future big days for some time.

The recipes are designed so that you can make a dog friendly version of your favorite dessert or so that you can make a people pleasing version of your dog's treat! In each recipe, you'll see two columns (see figure below) - one "For Maeby" (or your pup) and one "For Me" (that's you!). Whether you make one or both versions, it's important to make a note of the differences in ingredients, as dogs cannot eat everything we can.

If you are not sure where to begin, the "Where to Start" flowchart (pg. 12) can point you to recipe suggestions based on you or your dog's favorite ingredients.

Please note that before giving your dog any treats, it's important to check with your veterinarian and test your pup's reaction by feeding them only a little bit at first.

Most of all, have fun! For most of us, it's difficult to find time to bake for fun and very rare that we get to enjoy it with our furry companions, so enjoy the sweet (or savory) moments you get to create with them.

Also, be sure to share your experiences with us on Instagram (@muppetmaeby and @maebyandmecookbook). We look forward to making lots of new friends and experiencing your baking adventures too!

Enjoy!

CAROB CHIPS

CHOCOLATE CHIPS

PEANUT BUTTER OATMEAL "CHOCOLATE" CHIP COOKIES

This soft, chewy, and addictive cookie was the inspiration for this entire book! Maeby and I first baked these on a lazy Sunday, combining one of my favorite recipes with one of her favorite treats, peanut butter! As we enjoyed the cookies together, the photo of us inspired me to think that maybe there are enough dog friendly recipes to create a complete cookbook.

These cookies are an easy go-to treat for everyone, and as long as you have carob chips and all-natural peanut butter, you likely already have all those ingredients in your pantry. (In a pinch, you could easily make the dog cookies without carob chips, and they would be just as happy.) They really are the perfect cookie for a weekend baking whim.

Note: If you plan to make both recipes simultaneously, I recommend beginning with the human cookies.

FOR MAEBY — Makes 24

1 cup old fashioned oats
1 cup all natural peanut butter
¼ cup honey
1 egg
¼ teaspoon baking soda
¼ cup carob chips

1. Preheat oven to 325°F.
2. In a medium bowl, combine the oats, peanut butter, honey, egg, and baking soda.
3. Form teaspoon sized dough balls onto a parchment paper lined baking sheet. Press a few carob chips into the top for decoration.
4. Bake for 5-8 minutes until edges are firm. Allow to cool on a baking sheet for 2-3 minutes before transferring to a wire rack to cool completely.

Make sure to use CAROB CHIPS in your pup's cookies, not chocolate chips!

FOR ME — Makes 24

2½ cups old fashioned oats
1 cup flour
1 teaspoon baking powder
1 teaspoon baking soda
1 teaspoon salt
1 cup unsalted butter, softened
1 cup white sugar
½ cup brown sugar (I prefer dark brown sugar)
2 large eggs
1 cup peanut butter
2 teaspoons vanilla
2 cups semi sweet chocolate chips

1. Preheat the oven to 350°F (325°F if preparing both recipes simultaneously).
2. In a medium bowl, combine the oats, flour, baking powder, baking soda, and salt.
3. In a large bowl, cream together the butter, white sugar, and brown sugar. Beat in the eggs, peanut butter, and vanilla.
4. Add the dry ingredients to the large bowl and mix until combined.
5. Fold in the chocolate chips.
6. Cover and chill dough for 20 minutes.
7. (Prepare & bake MAEBY's recipe here if baking both simultaneously. When completed, preheat oven to 350°F.)
8. Form 1½ sized dough balls on parchment paper lined baking sheets. Bake 12-14 minutes or until edges have lightly browned. (Cookies may appear underbaked.)
9. Allow to cool for 5 minutes on baking sheets, and then transfer to wire rack.

Safety First: Only serve to your pup once completely cool to the touch

DOG FRIENDLY INGREDIENTS

While some of our favorite ingredients are just fine to share with our dogs and can even provide some health benefits to them, we have to remember that other ingredients can be very harmful. Therefore, it is common to have dog friendly recipes in order to keep our dogs safe. Be careful not to mix up or cross contaminate similar looking ingredients like chocolate chips and carob chips. Chocolate is very harmful to dogs, while carob is perfectly ok! Other common foods that you shouldn't feed your pup are grapes, raisins, avocado, apple seeds/core, peach pit, onion, and raw dough. As regularly noted throughout the recipes, if you're unsure about something, be sure to ask your veterinarian.

Ingredients shown on right (left to right, top to bottom): honey, blueberries/raspberries, cinnamon, carob chips, egg, cheese, peanut butter, dog biscuits, apple, banana, carrots, oats

WHERE TO START

When creating recipes for Maeby, I often began with one or two ingredients that she loves. What does your dog love?!

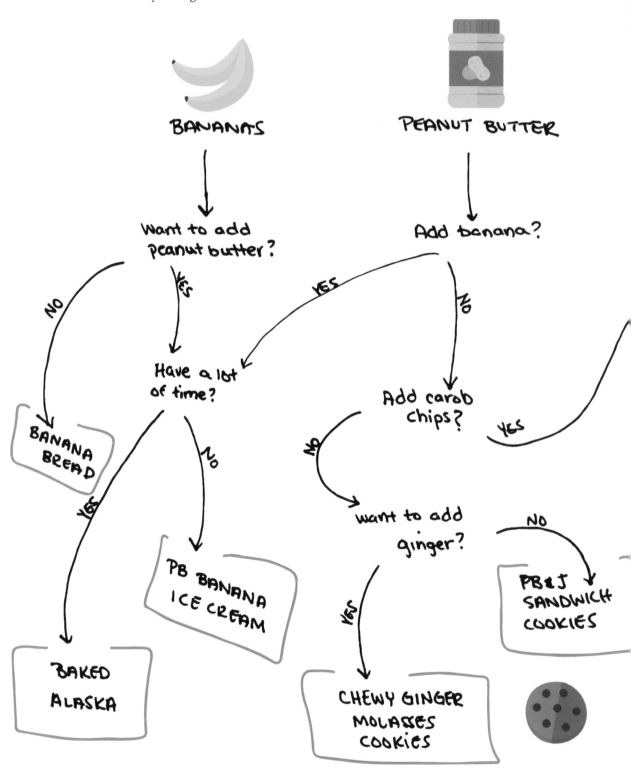

BANANAS

PEANUT BUTTER

Want to add peanut butter?

Add banana?

NO

YES

YES

NO

Have a lot of time?

Add carob chips?

YES

BANANA BREAD

NO

NO

want to add ginger?

NO

PB&J SANDWICH COOKIES

YES

PB BANANA ICE CREAM

YES

BAKED ALASKA

CHEWY GINGER MOLASSES COOKIES

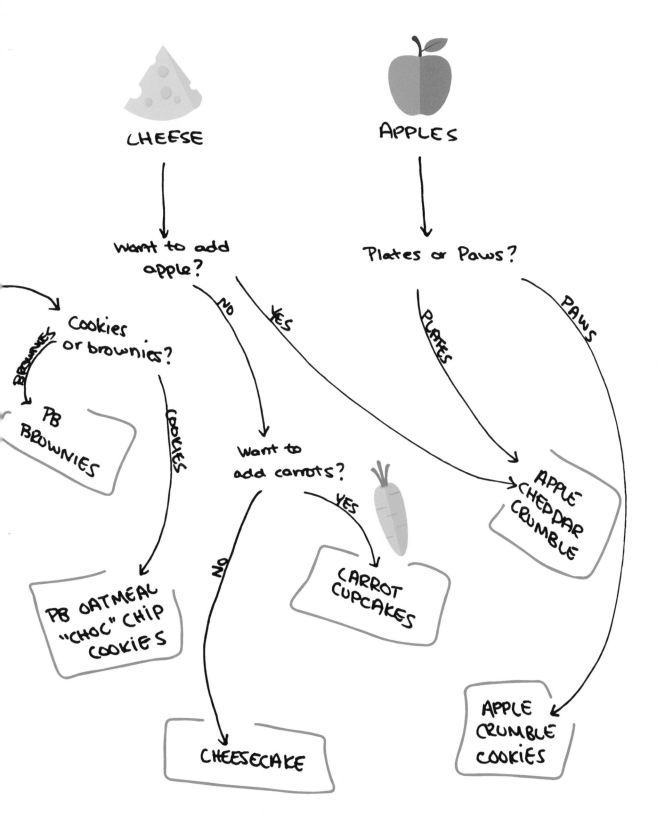

CHEESE

APPLES

Want to add apple?

Plates or Paws?

NO

YES

PLATES

PAWS

Cookies or brownies?

BROWNIES

COOKIES

PB BROWNIES

Want to add carrots?

YES

NO

APPLE CHEDDAR CRUMBLE

PB OATMEAL "CHOC" CHIP COOKIES

CARROT CUPCAKES

APPLE CRUMBLE COOKIES

CHEESECAKE

COOKIES & BROWNIES

Chewy Ginger Molasses Cookies (pg. 19)

CAROB CHIPS

CHOCOLATE CHIPS

PEANUT BUTTER OATMEAL "CHOCOLATE" CHIP COOKIES

This soft, chewy, and addictive cookie was the inspiration for this entire book! Maeby and I first baked these on a lazy Sunday, combining one of my favorite recipes with one of her favorite treats, peanut butter! As we enjoyed the cookies together, the photo of us inspired me to think that maybe there are enough dog friendly recipes to create a complete cookbook.

These cookies are an easy go-to treat for everyone, and as long as you have carob chips and all-natural peanut butter, you likely already have all these ingredients in your pantry. (In a pinch, you could easily make the dog cookies without carob chips, and they would be just as happy.) They really are the perfect cookie for a weekend baking whim.

Note: If you plan to make both recipes simultaneously, I recommend beginning with the human cookies.

FOR MAEBY   *Makes 24*

1 cup old fashioned oats
1 cup all natural peanut butter
½ cup honey
1 egg
⅛ teaspoon baking soda
¼ cup carob chips

1. Preheat oven to 325°F.

2. In a medium bowl, combine the oats, peanut butter, honey, egg, and baking soda.

3. Form teaspoon sized dough balls onto a parchment paper lined baking sheet. Press a few carob chips into the top for decoration.

4. Bake for 5-8 minutes until edges are firm. Allow to cool on a baking sheet for 2-3 minutes before transferring to a wire rack to cool completely.

Make sure to use CAROB CHIPS in your pup's cookies, not chocolate chips!

FOR ME   *Makes 24*

2 ½ cups old fashioned oats
1 cup flour
1 teaspoon baking powder
1 teaspoon baking soda
1 teaspoon salt
1 cup unsalted butter, softened
1 cup white sugar
½ cup brown sugar (I prefer dark brown sugar)
2 large eggs
1 cup peanut butter
2 teaspoons vanilla
2 cups semi-sweet chocolate chips

1. Preheat the oven to 350°F (325°F if preparing both recipes simultaneously).

2. In a medium bowl, combine the oats, flour, baking powder, baking soda, and salt.

3. In a large bowl, cream together the butter, white sugar, and brown sugar. Beat in the eggs, peanut butter, and vanilla.

4. Add the dry ingredients to the large bowl and mix until combined.

5. Fold in the chocolate chips.

6. Cover and chill dough for 20 minutes.

7. (Prepare & bake MAEBY's recipe here if baking both simultaneously. When completed, preheat oven to 350°F.)

8. Form 1 ½" sized dough balls on parchment paper lined baking sheets. Bake 12-14 minutes or until edges have lightly browned.
    (Cookies may appear underbaked.)

9. Allow to cool for 5 minutes on baking sheets, and then transfer to wire rack.

Safety First: Only serve to your pup once completely cool to the touch

CHEWY GINGER MOLASSES COOKIES

If a cookie could be cozy, this would be that cookie. These chewy, spicy cookies are a perfect winter treat and will be a hit at all your holiday parties. So why not let the pups celebrate too?! Being one of my favorite cookies, I, of course, made a point to make a dog version. Initially, I was very skeptical of what seems to be an intensely bitter pup version, but to my surprise, Maeby is obsessed with these.

Though the dog cookies are as easy as any other cookie, the human cookies' sparkly exterior requires each dough ball be rolled in raw sugar. To save some time, you can make the dough in advance and store it in plastic wrap or an airtight container in the refrigerator for up to three days. Just make sure it has some time to soften before baking.

Note: If you plan to make both recipes simultaneously, I recommend beginning with the human cookies.

FOR MAEBY   *Makes 24*

1 cup flour
⅓ cup all natural peanut butter
1 egg
2 tablespoons dark molasses
2 teaspoons ground ginger
1 teaspoon ground cinnamon

1. Preheat the oven to 320°F.

2. In a medium bowl, combine the flour, peanut butter, egg, molasses, ginger, and cinnamon.

3. Form into nickel-sized discs about ¼ inch thick and place on a parchment lined baking sheet. (If the dough is too sticky, cover and chill for 10-20 minutes.)

4. Bake for 15 minutes or until edges are firm. (These cookies will not look much different when ready, so be sure not to over bake, as they will get hard and crunchy.)

5. Transfer to a wire rack and let cool.

FOR ME   *Makes 24*

2 cups flour
2 teaspoons baking soda
1 ½ teaspoons ground cinnamon
1 teaspoon ground ginger
½ teaspoon ground cloves
½ teaspoon salt
½ cup unsalted butter, melted
⅓ cup white sugar
⅓ cup dark molasses
¼ cup light brown sugar
1 large egg
Raw sugar for coating (about ½ cup)

1. Preheat oven to 375°F (320°F if preparing both recipes simultaneously).

2. In a medium bowl, whisk together flour, baking soda, cinnamon, ginger, cloves, and salt. Set aside.

3. In a large bowl, whisk sugar, molasses, brown sugar, & egg into melted butter. Add dry ingredients and mix until combined.

4. Cover and chill for 20 minutes.

5. (Prepare & bake MAEBY's recipe here if baking both simultaneously. Preheat oven to 375°F when complete.)

6. Roll tablespoon-sized balls and coat in raw sugar. Place 2 inches apart on a parchment lined baking sheet.

7. Bake for 8-10 minutes. Cookies should be puffed, cracked, and have set edges.

8. Transfer to wire rack immediately and let cool.

Safety First: Only serve these to your pup once they are completely cool!

PEANUT BUTTER DEEP DISH BROWNIES

Inspired by one of my junior high school teachers, these brownies have been a staple in my household for over 15 years. I was lucky enough to attend a junior high school that made life skill electives mandatory for all students. It had never occurred to me that others were learning these skills for the first time since I grew up in a household where I was constantly learning about woodworking, sewing, cooking, and all things artsy. Her class felt like an extension of my home in some ways,

so I'm glad that a piece of it has stuck with me this long.

After recently discovering carob, I immediately thought of making a dog friendly version of these brownies. I wasn't convinced Maeby would like this, so I went ahead and added peanut butter to the recipe to ensure she'd at least try it. One bite in and she looked right past the peanut butter, asking for more before she'd even cleaned the remaining drizzle on the plate.

Note: Be extra careful when making these, as you would never want to mix up carob powder and cocoa powder.

FOR MAEBY   *Makes 10*

¼ cup honey
3 tablespoons vegetable oil
1 egg
¼ cup flour
3 tablespoons carob powder
Pinch of baking powder
All-natural peanut butter for drizzling

1. Preheat oven to 350°F.

2. In a medium mixing bowl, beat together honey, oil, and egg.

3. In separate bowl, combine flour, carob powder, and baking powder.

4. Stir flour mixture into the liquid mixture until combined.

5. Pour batter into greased or lined miniature baking pan (6"x3") or cupcake tin. Bake 20-25 minutes or until toothpick comes out of the center almost clean. (Bake times may vary depending on the size and type of baking pan.)

6. Drizzle with peanut butter.

FOR ME   *Makes 9*

1 ½ cup sugar
¾ cup unsalted butter, melted
3 eggs
1 ½ teaspoon vanilla
¾ cup flour
½ cocoa powder
½ teaspoon baking powder
½ teaspoon salt
6 oz. semi-sweet chocolate chips or peanut butter chips
All-natural peanut butter for drizzling

1. Preheat oven to 350°F. Grease square 8x8x2 pan.

2. In a large mixing bowl, beat together sugar, butter, eggs, and vanilla.

3. In separate bowl, combine flour, cocoa, baking powder, and salt.

4. Stir flour mixture into the butter/sugar mixture until combined. Fold in chocolate chips or peanut butter chips.

5. Bake up to 45 minutes or until toothpick comes out of the center almost clean.

6. Drizzle with peanut butter.

Safety First: Only serve these to your pup once they are completely cool!

APPLE CRUMBLE COOKIES

For when you don't have quite enough time to make a full apple crumble, these quick cookies will easily satisfy your apple crumble craving in half the time and are easy to pack on the go. Inspired by the Apple Cheddar Crumble (pg. 41), these chewy, crunchy, sweet, and savory cookies were created in order to satisfy our love for constant snacking.

FOR MAEBY   *Makes 24*

¼ cup honey
½ egg, beaten (about 2 tablespoons)
¾ cup old fashioned oats
½ cup flour + some for rolling
¼ teaspoon ground cinnamon
¼ cup diced Granny Smith apple
(about ¼ an apple)

1. Preheat the oven to 350°F.

2. In a medium bowl, combine the honey, egg, oats, flour, and cinnamon.

3. Fold in the apple chunks.

4. Roll out dough so that it's ¼" thick and use small cookie cutters to make 1-1 ½ inch sized treats. (Add flour as needed and/or refrigerate 10-20 minute to make it a little easier to work with.)

5. Place onto a parchment lined baking sheet and bake for 8-10 minutes or until golden brown.

6. Transfer to wire rack to cool completely before serving.

FOR ME   *Makes 24*

¾ cup unsalted butter, softened
¾ cup brown sugar
¾ cup white sugar
1 large egg
1 teaspoon vanilla
2 cups old fashioned oats
1 cup flour
1 teaspoon ground cinnamon
½ teaspoon ground nutmeg
½ teaspoon ground allspice
½ teaspoon baking soda
½ teaspoon salt
½ cup diced Granny Smith apple (about ½ an apple)

1. Preheat the oven to 350°F.

2. In a large bowl, combine the butter, sugars, egg, and vanilla.

3. In a separate bowl, whisk together the oats, flour, cinnamon, nutmeg, allspice, baking soda, and salt. Add this mixture to the butter and sugar mixture and stir until combined.

4. Fold in the apple chunks.

5. Drop heaping tablespoon sized balls of dough onto a parchment lined baking sheet and bake for 12-15 minutes or until golden brown. (If dough is too sticky, you can refrigerate it for 10-20 minutes to make it a little easier to work with.)

6. Allow cookies to cool for a few minutes on the baking sheet, then transfer to a wire rack to cool completely.

Safety First: Only serve these to your pup once they are completely cool!

PUMPKIN "CHOCOLATE" CHIP COOKIES

A nice fall twist on traditional chocolate chip cookie, this cookie is a seasonal favorite among dogs and people. Traditionally, canned pumpkin is understood to be a sort of miracle food for dogs, as it helps with digestion and upset tummies. Unfortunately (or fortunately) for me, Maeby has other opinions and has never liked pumpkin, leaving all the pumpkins cookies in the world to us and our less finicky four-legged friends.

FOR MAEBY   *Makes 24*

¾ cup flour
⅛ teaspoon baking soda
⅛ teaspoon cinnamon
1 tbsp honey
2 tbsp cup butter, melted
1 egg yolk
¼ cup canned pumpkin purée
¼ cup carob chips

1. Preheat oven to 350°F.

2. In a small bowl, combine flour, baking soda, and cinnamon. Set aside.

3. In a separate bowl, combine honey, butter, egg yolk, and pumpkin.

4. Mix flour mixture into pumpkin mixture until combined. Fold in carob chips.

5. Cover and refrigerate dough for 20 minutes if really tacky.

6. On a parchment lined baking sheet, roll approximately ½ inch sized dough balls and flatten so they are about the size of quarters.

7. Bake for 5-7 minutes.

8. Cool on wire racks and store in an airtight container.

Make sure to use CAROB CHIPS in your pup's cookies, not chocolate chips!

FOR ME   *Makes 18*

1 ½ cups flour
½ teaspoon baking soda
½ teaspoon salt
1 teaspoon cinnamon
¼ teaspoon nutmeg
¼ teaspoon allspice
½ cup white sugar
½ cup brown sugar
½ cup butter, browned
1 egg yolk
½ cup pumpkin purée
3/4 cup semi-sweet chocolate chips

1. Preheat oven to 350°F.

2. In a medium bowl, combine flour, baking soda, salt, cinnamon, nutmeg, and allspice. Set aside.

3. In a large bowl, combine sugars and butter. Add egg yolk and pumpkin and mix until combined.

4. Gradually mix in flour mixture until combined. Fold in chocolate chips.

5. Cover and refrigerate dough for 20 minutes.

6. Drop heaping tablespoonfuls onto parchment lined cookie sheet.

7. Bake for 12-15 minutes or until edges begin to brown.

8. Cool on wire racks and store in an airtight container.

PEANUT BUTTER & JELLY SANDWICH COOKIES

After the hundreds of times I've seen Maeby waiting patiently (and sometimes not so patiently) over the top of my peanut butter and jelly sandwiches, she finally has a PB&J made just for her. Peanut butter seems to be every dog's weakness, so I'm sure many of you are familiar with the gentle tap of their paw or challenge to engage in a staring contest (that we rarely win) to make their PB&J dreams come true.

Unlike other recipes, I designed the dog version of this treat first. When short on time, a simpler version can be made by making them into thumbprint cookies instead of sandwiches – an easy process that can be done by pressing your thumb into a dough ball and filling it with jam before baking.

These are incredibly easy and take very little time, so experiment with small batches (pg. 28) and different jams if you wish, just make sure they remain safe for your pup!

FOR MAEBY   *Makes 40*

1 cup all-natural peanut butter
1 egg
4 tablespoons strawberry or raspberry purée
Flour for rolling

1. Preheat oven to 350°F.

2. In a medium bowl, mix together peanut butter & egg until well blended.

3. Roll out dough on lightly floured surface to ¼ inch thick and cut 1 inch round cookies. (For thumbprints, instead of sandwiches, roll ½ inch dough balls and press your thumb in the center and add ½ teaspoon of fruit purée.)

4. Place onto parchment lined cookie sheet and bake for 7 to 10 minutes.

5. Allow to cool for 5 minutes on the cookie sheet before transferring to wire racks to cool completely. Cookies will harden while cooling.

6. Store peanut butter cookies in an airtight container for up to 1 week.

7. When serving, sandwich the fruit purée between two cookies (about ½ teaspoon each).

FOR ME   *Makes 12*

1 cup peanut butter
1 cup white sugar
1 egg
½ teaspoon vanilla extract
¼ teaspoon salt
8 tablespoons fruit preserves
Flour for rolling

1. Preheat oven to 350°F.

2. In a medium bowl, mix together peanut butter, sugar, egg, vanilla, and salt until well blended.

3. Roll out dough on lightly floured surface to ¼ inch thick and cut 1 ½ inch round cookies. (For thumbprints, instead of sandwiches, roll 1 inch dough balls and press your thumb in the center and add a teaspoon of preserves.)

4. Place onto parchment lined cookie sheet and bake for 8 to 11 minutes or until the edges are set.

5. Allow to cool for 5 minutes on the cookie sheet before transferring to wire racks to cool completely. Cookies will harden while cooling.

6. Store peanut butter cookies in an airtight container for up to 1 week.

7. When serving, sandwich the fruit preserves between two cookies (about 1 teaspoon each).

FOR MAEBY & ME

1 cup all-natural peanut butter
½ cup white sugar
1 egg
¼ teaspoon vanilla extract
⅛ teaspoon salt
4 tablespoons fruit preserves
2 tablespoons strawberry or raspberry purée
Flour for rolling

1. Preheat oven to 350°F.

2. In a medium bowl, mix together peanut butter and egg.

3. Set ½ of the mixture aside in a small bowl. This is your pup's cookie dough!

4. Roll out the pup friendly dough on a lightly floured surface to ¼ inch thick and cut 1 inch round cookies. (For thumbprints, instead of sandwiches, roll ½ inch dough balls and press your thumb in the center and add ½ teaspoon of fruit purée.)

5. Place onto parchment lined cookie sheet and bake for 7 to 10 minutes.

6. While the pup cookies are baking, add sugar, vanilla, and salt to the remaining mixture in the medium bowl and stir until combined.

7. Roll out dough on a lightly floured surface to ¼ inch thick and cut 1 ½ inch round cookies. (For thumbprints, instead of sandwiches, roll 1 inch dough balls and press your thumb in the center and add a teaspoon of preserves.)

8. Place onto parchment lined cookie sheet and bake for 8 to 11 minutes or until the edges are set.

9. Allow both types of cookies to cool for 5 minutes on the cookie sheet before transferring to wire racks to cool completely. Cookies will harden while cooling.

10. Store peanut butter cookies in an airtight container for up to 1 week.

11. When serving, sandwich 1 teaspoon of the fruit preserves (for you) or ½ teaspoon of the fruit purée (for your pup!) between two cookies.

COCONUT MACAROONS

Admittedly, Maeby was the one demanding that these make it into the book, as I've never really craved coconut. After enjoying some doggie friendly granola that featured coconut at a new dog cafe in our neighborhood, I made it a goal to find ways for us to both enjoy it and came up with these macaroons!

Though they may not be the most sophisticated macaroons out there, they are very easy to make and we've certainly enjoyed them!

FOR MAEBY
Makes 24

1 cup unsweetened coconut flakes
1 egg white
1 tablespoon honey

1. Preheat oven to 350°F.

2. In a medium bowl, combine egg whites and honey. Fold in coconut flakes.

3. Scoop even sized mounds onto parchment lined cookie sheet. Size of the mounds can range from ½ inch to 1 inch depending on the size of your dog.
(I use a ½ teaspoon per cookie.)

4. Bake for 8-12 minutes or until they start to lightly brown.

5. Remove from the oven and let cool on the cookie sheet for 10 minutes. Transfer to wire rack to finish cooling.

FOR ME
Makes 24

2 cups sweetened coconut flakes
2 egg whites
2 tablespoons white sugar (or honey)
½ teaspoon vanilla

1. Preheat oven to 350°F.

2. In a large bowl, combine egg whites, sugar, and vanilla. Fold in coconut flakes.

3. Use a mini ice cream scoop or melon baller to scoop tablespoon sized mounds onto parchment lined cookie sheet.

4. Bake for 10-15 minutes or until the tops start to lightly brown.

5. Remove from the oven and let cool on the cookie sheet for 10 minutes. Transfer to wire rack to finish cooling.

HOW WE MET

On August 17, 2013, I adopted Maeby at three months old. I had looked for a dog to rescue for about 8 months, but being in my late 20's with a career that had me traveling often, it was difficult to find a dog that would be compatible with my lifestyle. I dreamt of a laid-back dog that I could get at a young age, so I could train her myself, and would remain small enough to fly with me. I wanted an athletic dog, but hopefully not one that would shed much (or at all).

I couldn't imagine what she looked like even if I tried, and I knew my wish list was already a tall order.

In the week leading up to August 17, 2013, I had learned that a dog I was interested in was going to another family. I had high hopes and was pretty disappointed to say the least. But that Saturday morning, I took an unplanned detour to an adoption event on the way to the grocery store. I had no intention of adopting a dog; I really just wanted to play with a dog that also may have

needed some cheering up. The event was chaotic - so loud that I am not sure why I didn't leave right away. But amidst the chaos of many dogs barking loudly from their crates was the most adorable puppy I had seen all year, sleeping through all the madness in her own crate right in the center.

I asked to take that pup for a walk (as I had done with many adoptable dogs in the past) and knew immediately that she was the dog I'd been looking for. I stopped periodically to try and observe her, but each time we stopped, she would simply sit on my feet and look up at me, waiting patiently, like I had directions for her. She was calm, sweet, smart, eager to learn, and somehow checked all the boxes of my unrealistic wish list. Most importantly, I seemed to check off all her boxes too. I was so overjoyed and overwhelmed by how everything seemed to have worked out as it was meant to. Maeby & I were a team right away (and I never made it to the grocery store that day).

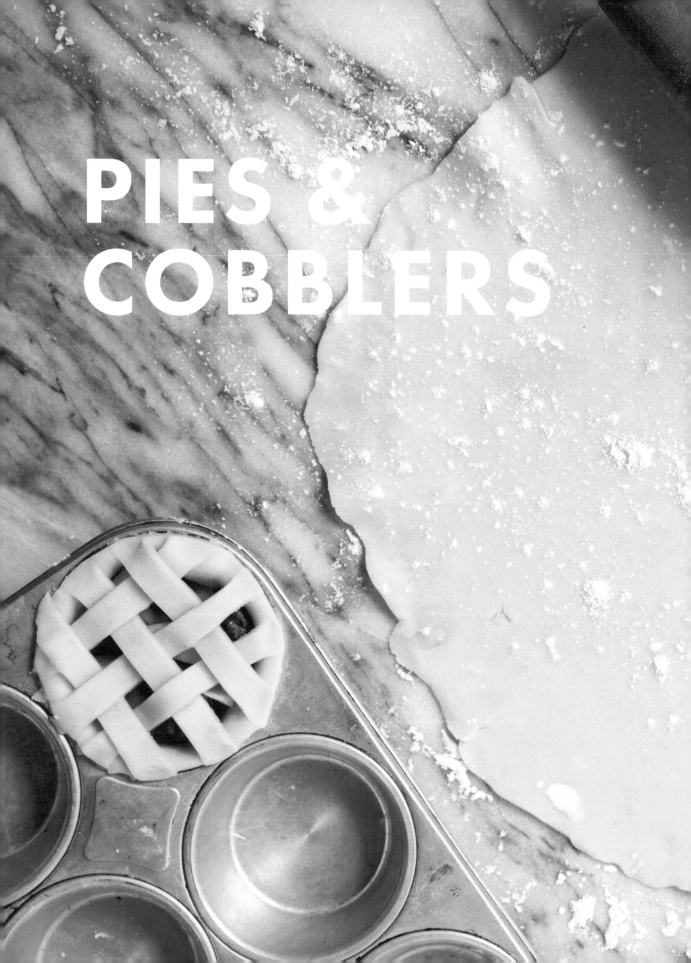

PIES &
COBBLERS

Peach Blueberry Pie (pg. 43)

SWEET POTATO PIE

This pie is for the discerning dog in your life, one that is always looking for alternatives. Maeby's dislike of pumpkin was one of the first signs that she'd be a very opinionated dog – coupled with her love of couch cushions, her hatred of hardwood floors, her variety of expressions, and her love of chasing pigeons & seagulls – but not other birds. Regardless, it all led to this amazing sweet potato pie! Though I don't mind a good pumpkin pie myself, I think sweet potato pies are definitely underrated. Enjoy this one with a little whipped cream (just for you) or a drizzle of honey (for both of you!).

FOR MAEBY

Serves 4
Makes one 5" mini pie or two 3" cupcake sized pies

For the crust:
2 tablespoons cold butter, cut into pieces
¼ cup + 1 tablespoon flour (and some for rolling)
2 tablespoons cold water

For the filling:
¼ lb sweet potatoes (or ½ cup mashed sweet potatoes)
⅛ cup evaporated milk
2 tablespoons egg, beaten (approx. ½ egg, beaten)
1 teaspoon molasses
½ teaspoon flour

1. Preheat the oven to 325°F.

2. Roast foil wrapped sweet potatoes for 2 hours or until a fork or knife easily goes through the center. (For sweeter potatoes, roast longer at lower temperatures or put potatoes in the oven while it's still preheating. For quicker potatoes, roast for 1 hour at 400°F or boil until soft.) Set potatoes aside to cool.

3. While the potatoes are roasting, make the crust. Cut butter into flour until the mixture resembles breadcrumbs.

4. Slowly add cold water until mixture resembles a ball of dough. Wrap in plastic wrap and chill in the refrigerator.

5. Make the Filling: Adjust/preheat the oven temperature to 350°F.

6. Remove the skins and whisk potatoes (medium setting) until smooth.

7. Add evaporated milk, egg, molasses, & flour and whisk until smooth.

8. Roll out your pie crust to a 5" circle or two 3" circles and line mini pie dish or two compartments of a cupcake tin, pressing down the edges and cutting away any excess.

9. Pour filling into pie crust and bake for 30-40 minutes or until the center is set and the crust has browned. (If the edges of the crust start to get too brown, cover them with a crust shield or aluminum foil to prevent further browning.)

10. Allow pie to cool completely, wrap, and store in the refrigerator.

FOR ME

For the crust:
½ cup shortening (or cold butter, cut into pieces)
1 ¼ cups flour (and some for rolling)
½ teaspoon salt
¼ cup cold water

For the filling:
1 lb sweet potatoes (or 2 cups mashed sweet potatoes)
½ cup butter, softened
1 cup brown sugar
½ cup evaporated milk
2 eggs
1 teaspoon vanilla
½ teaspoon cinnamon
¼ teaspoon ginger
¼ teaspoon nutmeg
2 teaspoons flour

1. Preheat the oven to 325°F.

2. Roast foil wrapped sweet potatoes for 2 hours or until a fork or knife easily goes through the center. (For sweeter potatoes, roast longer at lower temperatures or put potatoes in the oven while it's still preheating. For quicker potatoes, roast for 1 hour at 400°F.) Set potatoes aside to cool.

3. While the potatoes are roasting, make the crust. Combine flour and salt. Cut in shortening until the mixture resembles breadcrumbs.

4. Slowly add cold water until mixture resembles a ball of dough. Wrap in plastic wrap and chill in the refrigerator.

5. Make the Filling: Adjust/preheat the oven temperature to 350°F.

6. Remove the skins and whisk potatoes and butter (medium setting) until smooth.

7. Add brown sugar, evaporated milk, eggs, vanilla, cinnamon, ginger, nutmeg, & flour and whisk until smooth.

8. Roll out your pie crust to a 9" circle and line a pie dish, pressing down the edges and cutting away any excess.

9. Pour filling into pie crust and bake for 55-60 minutes or until the center is set. (If the edges of the crust start to get too brown, cover them with a crust shield or aluminum foil to prevent further browning.

10. Allow pie to cool a bit and serve warm or cool completely, wrap, and store in the refrigerator.

APPLE CHEDDAR CRUMBLE

This recipe came to life while trying to find more desserts that catered to our mutual love of cheese. Soon after, on our first trip to Cape Cod, we heard about the New England & English tradition of putting a slice of cheese on apple pie and developed this dog friendly crumble that very weekend.

Cheese and pie together might sound strange at first, but after taste testing with and without cheese, it's clear that the cheese brings that magical sweet and savory combo that many of us love, like when you share a fruit, cheese, and nut platter. If you're feeling really bold, you might just add a full slice of cheese right on top.

Note: If you plan to make both recipes, they can be prepared side by side and baked together.

FOR MAEBY   *Serves 4*

For the filling:
1 medium Granny Smith apple, peeled & chopped
1 teaspoon honey

For the crumb topping:
2 tablespoons flour
3 tablespoons old-fashioned rolled oats
2 teaspoons honey
1 tablespoon cheddar cheese, shredded
1 tablespoon unsalted butter

1. Preheat oven to 375°F.

2. In a small bowl, combine the crumb topping ingredients with a fork until it resembles small crumbs. Refrigerate while you prepare the apple filling.

3. In a medium size bowl, toss peeled, cored, and chopped apple in honey.

4. Pour apple mixture into a 5 inch custard dish/mini pie tin and gently press it down. (If you don't have a 5 inch baking dish, feel free to use a cupcake tin. You will have enough filling and topping to make multiple cupcake sized crumbles.)

5. Sprinkle crumb topping evenly over the apples. (Topping may become clumpy. Simply break it back up when topping the filling.)

6. Bake for 20-30 minutes or until golden brown.

7. Allow to cool completely before serving.

8. Serve with pup friendly frozen yogurt or ice cream if desired.

FOR ME   *Serves 8*

For the filling:
6 medium Granny Smith apples, peeled & thinly sliced
2 tablespoons lemon juice
¼ cup dark brown sugar
¼ teaspoon ground cinnamon
¼ teaspoon nutmeg

For the crumb topping:
⅓ cup cheddar cheese, shredded
½ cup flour
¾ cup old-fashioned rolled oats
½ cup dark brown sugar
⅓ cup unsalted butter, softened

1. Preheat oven to 375°F.

2. In a medium size bowl combine the crumb topping ingredients with a fork until it resembles small crumbs. Refrigerate while you prepare the apple filling.

3. In a large bowl, toss peeled, cored, and thinly sliced apples in lemon juice, brown sugar, cinnamon, and nutmeg.

4. Pour apple mixture into an 8x8-inch baking dish and gently press it down.

5. Sprinkle crumb topping evenly over the apples.

6. Bake for 30-35 minutes or until golden brown and top is set.

7. Allow to cool for at least 10 minutes before serving.

8. Serve with ice cream or frozen yogurt if desired.

PEACH BLUEBERRY PIE

Inspired by Maeby's love of blueberries and an incredible pie my cousin made for a family gathering, this dog recipe was designed specially for Maeby's 5th birthday. Though she was initially a bit confused by the crust, treating it more like a bowl than food, she did enjoy cleaning out the pie's filling.

Without a mini pie tin, I used a cupcake or muffin tin to make this mini pie. It was so successful and easy that I might consider making myself some mini pies this way in the future!

Note: If making both recipes, all steps can be done simultaneously!

FOR MAEBY
Serves 4
Makes one 5" mini pie or two 3" cupcake sized pies

For the crust:
4 tablespoons cold butter, cut into pieces
½ cup + 1 tablespoon flour (and some for rolling)
4 tablespoons cold water
1 egg, beaten (if making both recipes, 1 egg can be shared across both recipes)

For the filling:
¼ cup fresh blueberries
1 fresh peach
2 tablespoons honey

1. Make the Crust: Cut butter into flour with your fingers and add water. Form into ball, wrap in plastic, and refrigerate.

2. Make the Filling: Preheat the oven to 400°F.

3. Peel and dice peach* & mix with blueberries and honey.

4. Split the dough in half. Roll out one half to fit a mini pie tin or muffin pan. Fill pie crust with peach/blueberry filling.

5. Roll out other half of dough and cut into strips to make lattice top. Press down around the edges, removing any excess pie dough. Brush the top of the lattice with a thin layer of the beaten egg.

6. Bake for 20 minutes or until golden brown.

7. Allow to cool completely on a wire rack. Cover and store in the refrigerator.

*Be careful to use only the flesh of the peach, as peach pits can be toxic to dogs

FOR ME
Serves 8

For the crust:
1 cup shortening (or cold butter, cut into pieces)
2 ½ cups flour (and some for rolling)
1 teaspoon salt
½ cup cold water
1 egg, beaten (if making both recipes, 1 egg can be shared across both recipes)

For the filling:
¾ cup white sugar
6 tablespoons flour
½ teaspoon ground cinnamon
¼ teaspoon allspice
3 cups sliced, peeled fresh peaches (about 5)
1 ½ cups fresh blueberries

1. Make the Crust: Mix flour and salt. Cut shortening into flour mixture with your fingers and add water. Form into ball, wrap in plastic, and refrigerate.

2. Make the Filling: Preheat the oven to 400°F.

3. Mix flour, sugar, allspice, and cinnamon. Peel and dice peach & fold with blueberries into mixture.

4. Roll out dough into two discs, and fit one of them into a 9-inch pie tin. Fill pie crust with filling.

5. Using the remaining disc, make lattice top and press down around the edges, removing any excess pie dough. Brush the top of the lattice with a thin layer of the beaten egg.

6. Bake 20 minutes at 400°F on a baking sheet, then an additional 30-35 minutes at 375°F.

7. Allow to cool completely on a wire rack. Cover and store in the refrigerator.

these a
just for

PUMPKIN PIE

Though Maeby's usual stance is anti-pumpkin, she seemed mildly interested in this pie! Considering the health benefits of canned pumpkin for dogs, this was a big win for us. If you have a finicky pup too, this pie might be the gateway to them giving plain canned pumpkin a real chance. And for those pups already in love with canned pumpkin, this pie is a dream!

FOR MAEBY

Serves 4
Makes one 5" mini pie or
two 3" cupcake-sized mini pies

For the crust:
2 tablespoons cold butter, cut into pieces
¼ cup + 1 tablespoon flour (and some for rolling)
2 tablespoons cold water

For the filling:
½ cup pumpkin purée
⅛ cup evaporated milk
2 tablespoons egg, beaten (approx. ½ egg, beaten)
1 teaspoon molasses

1. Make the Crust: Cut butter into flour until the mixture resembles breadcrumbs.

2. Slowly add cold water until mixture resembles a ball of dough. Wrap in plastic wrap and chill in the refrigerator.

3. Make the Filling: Preheat the oven to 350°F.

4. In a medium bowl, combine pumpkin, evaporated milk, egg, and molasses. Whisk until smooth.

5. Roll out your pie crust to a 5" circle or two 3" circles and line mini pie dish or two compartments of a cupcake tin, pressing down the edges and cutting away any excess.

6. Pour filling into pie crust and bake for 30-40 minutes or until the center is set and the crust has browned. (If the edges of the crust start to get too brown, cover them with a crust shield or aluminum foil to prevent further browning.)

7. Allow pie to cool completely, wrap, and store in the refrigerator.

FOR ME

Serves 8
Makes one 9" pie

For the crust
½ cup shortening (or cold butter, cut into pieces)
1 ¼ cups flour (and some for rolling)
½ teaspoon salt
¼ cup cold water

For the filling
2 cups pumpkin purée
1 cup brown sugar
½ cup evaporated milk
2 eggs
½ teaspoon cinnamon
¼ teaspoon allspice

1. Make the Crust: Combine flour and salt. Cut in shortening until the mixture resembles breadcrumbs.

2. Slowly add cold water until mixture resembles a ball of dough. Wrap in plastic wrap and chill in the refrigerator.

3. Make the Filling: Preheat the oven to 350°F.

4. In a large bowl, combine brown sugar, evaporated milk, pumpkin, eggs, cinnamon, and allspice. Whisk until smooth.

5. Roll out your pie crust to a 9" circle on a flour dusted surface and line a pie dish with your crust, pressing down the edges and cutting away any excess.

6. Pour filling into pie crust and bake for 55-60 minutes or until the center is set or a toothpick comes out of the center almost clean. (If the edges of the crust start to get too brown, cover them with a crust shield or aluminum foil to prevent further browning.)

7. Allow pie to cool a bit and serve warm or cool completely, wrap, and store in the refrigerator.

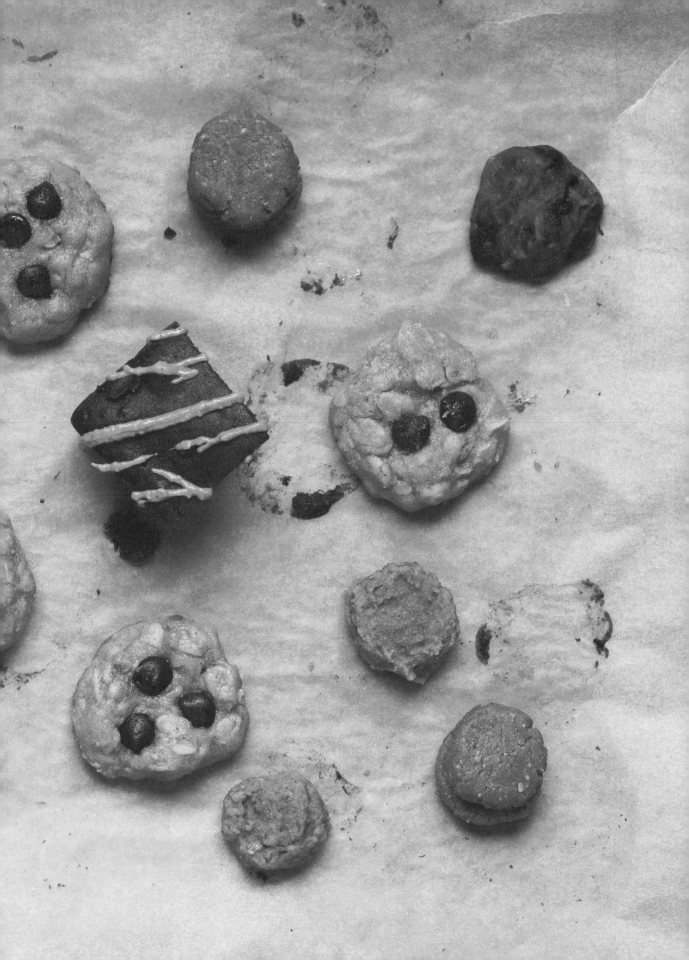

FROZEN TREATS

Strawberry Pineapple Frozen Yogurt (pg. 69)

STRAWBERRY PINEAPPLE FROZEN YOGURT

A refreshing treat for those hot, humid summer days, this frozen yogurt is one of Maeby's favorite summertime treats. A dairy addict, she usually comes running whenever she sees, hears, or smells yogurt, milk, or cheese nearby.

When I adopted Maeby, "froyo" was at the height of its trendiness. It was a regular treat for anyone looking for a guilt-free treat or relief from the summer heat. On Maeby's 3rd birthday, I started experimenting with dog friendly frozen yogurt, resulting in her peanut butter froyo "cake". Personally, I wanted something fruity and adjusted the recipe to a combo that we both like! Feel free to mess with the flavors or proportions to your liking, just be sure that you are only using dog safe ingredients.

Because frozen yogurt often gets very hard in the freezer, you may consider freezing frozen yogurt into individually portion sized silicone molds like the paw prints shown in Fruit "Pup"sicles (pg. 73).

Optional:
Be creative! Substitute the strawberries and pineapple juice for other dog friendly fruits like mangoes bananas, blueberries, raspberries, apples, or pears. For a savory twist, add peanut butter!

FOR MAEBY & ME   *Serves 4*

3 cups frozen strawberries
32 oz full fat Greek yogurt
⅓ cup honey
Splash of pineapple juice

1. Blend strawberries, yogurt, honey, and pineapple juice in food processor until smooth.

2. Spoon into popsicle molds or into a freezer safe dish and freeze for at least 2 hours.

PEANUT BUTTER BANANA ICE CREAM

Tired of using your overripe bananas to make banana bread? Try making this super simple banana "ice cream" that you can share with your pup instead!

For those of you on the hunt for healthy alternatives to ice cream, this recipe comes as no surprise. But for the rest of us, this recipe is mind blowing. I hesitated to include this in this book since it is so simple; however, since Maeby has a fondness for bananas and an obsession with peanut butter, I thought others might want to consider sharing this healthy snack with their pups too!

FOR MAEBY & ME

Serves 4

4 frozen, ripe to overripe bananas
¼ cup all natural peanut butter
Optional: splash of whole milk

1. Blend frozen, ripe to overripe bananas in a food processor until smooth.

2. When it starts to look like soft serve, add a splash of whole milk if you'd like a creamier texture.

3. Fold in peanut butter so some stripes of peanut butter remain.

4. Scoop and serve immediately or store in a freezer safe container.

FOR MAEBY:

Consider adding carob chips in addition or in lieu of the peanut butter.

FOR ME:

Consider adding chocolate chips, peanut butter chips, cinnamon, or strawberries

Note: The addition of chocolate chips or peanut butter chips would prevent this from being dog friendly.

cantaloupe

blueberr

Watermelon

MAEBY'S FAVORITE

FRUIT "PUP"SICLES

I often think of dogs as toddlers that never grow up, and for some reason toddlers go hand in hand with popsicles. Although Maeby is becoming more and more set in her ways, she still maintains her childlike enthusiasm while eating a "pup"sicle, sometimes even resulting in a brain freeze.

This summer treat is super easy to make, requiring only fresh fruit, a freezer, and a little bit of time. For a personal touch, use you and your pup's favorite flavors to mix and match different combinations.

FOR MAEBY   *Makes 2 – 4*

For Watermelon Pops:
1 cup seedless watermelon
¼ cup raspberries (about 6 raspberries)

For Blueberry Pops:
1 cup blueberries
1 tablespoon honey
Optional: ¼ cup plain yogurt

For Cantaloupe Pops:
1 cup cantaloupe
1 tablespoon honey

1. Add ingredients for desired flavor popsicle to a blender or food processor. Blend until smooth.

2. Fill silicone popsicle molds. If desired, insert rawhide as sticks about ¾ the way down. (Do not use regular popsicle sticks.) If you'd like to layer different flavors, fill the mold to the desired level and freeze before adding the next flavor.

3. Freeze for 3-4 hours or until completely frozen.

FOR ME   *Makes 12*

For Watermelon Pops:
5 cups seedless watermelon
½ cup raspberries
1 lime, juice of

For Blueberry Pops:
5 cups blueberries
½ cup honey
1 cup plain yogurt

For Cantaloupe Pops:
5 cups cantaloupe
⅓ cup honey
1 lemon, juice of

1. Add ingredients for desired flavor popsicle to a blender or food processor. Blend until smooth.

2. Fill popsicle molds and insert sticks about ¾ of the way. If you'd like to layer different flavors, fill the mold to the desired level and freeze before adding the next flavor.

3. Freeze for 3-4 hours or until completely frozen.

Safety First: "Pup"sicles should not have sticks unless they are edible and dog friendly.

TRAVELING WITH MAEBY

A well-traveled pup, Maeby has traveled by plane, train, automobile, and boat, visiting twenty U.S. states and the United Kingdom. Boarding at least two roundtrip flights per year, almost daily subway rides, a handful of cross-country road trips, and boat rides on two continents, she's always very excited to "come with," as I say to her, but treats always keep her spirits up on longer trips.

Chicago, IL

Santa Barbara, CA

Cedar Lake, IN

London, England

Oxford, England

New York City

123 Sesame Street

Oxford, England

DESSERTS THAT TRAVEL WELL

Chewy Ginger Molasses Cookies

Banana Bread

Peanut Butter Cookies (from Peanut Butter & Jelly Sandwich Cookies)

Peanut Butter Deep Dish Brownies

Peanut Butter Oatmeal "Chocolate" Chip Cookies

Coconut Macaroons

CAKES & BREADS

Carrot Cupcakes (pg. 81)

CARROT CUPCAKES

Maeby loves carrots, especially as her amuse-bouche before dinner. I love carrot cake, but I can never find the time to sit down and eat a whole cake. For those reasons, we both love these cupcakes. They're simple, look and taste great, and if you plan to save some for later, I find it's best to ice them just before serving.

If you have the time and are looking to make a statement, you can recreate the 6-inch triple layer carrot cake I made for her 6th birthday using this recipe. The mini cupcakes are just really cute and great for portion control.

FOR MAEBY

Makes 48

For the pupcakes:
2 cups flour
1 teaspoon baking soda
1 cup shredded carrots
2 tablespoons honey
3 tablespoons olive oil
2 large eggs
½ cup water

For the frosting:
8 ounces cream cheese, room temperature
2 tablespoons honey

1. Preheat the oven to 350°F. Line mini cupcake tin with liners and set aside.

2. In a medium bowl, combine flour and baking soda. Set aside.

3. In a large bowl, combine shredded carrots, honey, olive oil, eggs, and water. Add the dry ingredients from the medium bowl and mix until smooth.

4. Spoon into mini cupcake tin, filling each ⅔ of the way. Bake at 350°F for 20-25 minutes or until the tops of the cakes are set and a toothpick inserted into the center of each one comes out clean.

5. Remove from the oven, transfer to a wire rack, and allow to cool in the pans for about 10-15 minutes.

6. Once the cakes have cooled, remove from the pans and return the cakes to the wire rack to finish cooling.

7. In the bowl of a stand mixer fitted with the paddle attachment, or in a large mixing bowl using a hand-held mixer, beat the cream cheese until smooth. Add the honey and mix for about 30 seconds to 1 minute until well combined and smooth.

8. Frost the cupcakes using a spatula or with a piping bag.

For the cupcakes:
2 cups flour
2 teaspoons baking powder
1 teaspoon baking soda
1 ½ teaspoons ground cinnamon
¼ teaspoon ground ginger
¼ teaspoon ground nutmeg
½ teaspoon salt
¾ cup vegetable oil
4 large eggs, room temperature
1 cup dark brown sugar
1 cup white sugar
½ cup unsweetened applesauce
1 teaspoon vanilla extract
3 cups grated carrots, lightly packed

For the frosting:
1 (8-ounce) package cream cheese, softened to room temperature
½ cup unsalted butter, softened to room temperature
2-3 cups powdered sugar, to taste
2 teaspoons vanilla extract

1. Preheat oven to 350°F. Line cupcake tin with liners and set aside.

2. In a large mixing bowl, whisk together the flour, baking powder, baking soda, cinnamon, ginger, nutmeg, and salt until well combined. Set aside.

3. In a separate large mixing bowl, whisk together the oil, eggs, brown sugar, white sugar, applesauce, and vanilla extract until fully combined. Add the grated carrots and mix until well combined.

4. Pour the dry ingredients into the wet ingredients and mix with a whisk or rubber spatula until just combined, making sure not to over mix the batter.

5. Pour the cake batter into the cupcake tin, filling each ⅔ of the way. Bake at 350°F for 30-35 minutes or until the tops of the cakes are set and a toothpick inserted into the center of each one comes out clean.

6. Remove from the oven, transfer to a wire rack, and allow to cool in the pans for about 20-25 minutes. Once the cakes have cooled, remove from the pans and return the cakes to the wire rack to finish cooling.

7. In the bowl of a stand mixer fitted with the paddle attachment, or in a large mixing bowl using a hand-held mixer, beat the cream cheese until smooth. Add the butter and mix for about 30 seconds to 1 minute until well combined and smooth. Add in the powdered sugar and vanilla extract and continue mixing until fully combined, scraping down the sides of the bowl as needed.

8. Frost the cupcakes using a spatula or with a piping bag.

BANANA BREAD

After sharing a few bits of my bananas with Maeby over breakfast, I wanted to remember her when using up my overripe bananas as well. Banana bread has always been my go-to solution for overripe bananas, and it's a comforting, quick recipe requiring little to no preparation.

FOR MAEBY

Makes 1 mini loaf

1 ripe/overripe banana
1 teaspoon of milk
¼ teaspoon cinnamon
¼ cup honey
1 egg white
½ cup flour
Pinch of baking soda

1. Preheat oven to 350°F.

2. In a small bowl, mash banana with a fork and combine with milk and cinnamon.

3. Add honey and egg to the banana mixture.

4. In a medium bowl, combine flour and baking soda. Add dry ingredients to the banana mixture and stir until combined.

5. Pour batter into a greased mini bread pan and bake about 35-40 minutes or until top browns slightly and toothpick comes out of the center clean. Allow to cool in the pan.

FOR ME

Makes 1 loaf

3 ripe/overripe bananas
1 cup sugar
½ cup unsalted butter
2 large eggs
1 tablespoon milk
1 teaspoon cinnamon
2 cups flour
1 teaspoon baking soda
1 teaspoon baking powder
1 teaspoon salt

1. Preheat oven to 325°F.

2. In a large bowl, combine sugar, butter, and eggs.

3. In a small bowl, mash three bananas with a fork and combine with milk and cinnamon. Add banana mixture to sugar-butter-egg mixture.

4. In a medium bowl, combine flour, baking powder, baking soda, and salt. Add dry ingredients to the other mixture and stir until combined.

5. Pour batter into a greased bread pan and bake about 45-50 minutes or until a toothpick comes out of the center clean. Allow to cool in the pan.

dog bone
crust

CHEESECAKE

After taste testing my friend's cheesecakes in college, cheesecake has become my favorite cake. As an homage to his cakes and because Maeby's favorite human food is cheese, this was always high on my list to adapt for pups. If your pup is anything like Maeby, you're going to have to take this one away from them because they will just keep eating it.

FOR MAEBY   *Makes one 5" mini cheesecake*

1 cup ground dry dog biscuits
4 tablespoons butter, melted
1 - 8oz package cream cheese, softened
1 egg, slightly beaten
Raspberries or blueberries (optional)

Note: If you plan to make both recipes, begin this recipe while the human cheesecake is baking.

1. Preheat oven to 375°F.

2. Combine ground dog biscuits and melted butter. Press ¼ inch layer into bottom of mini cheesecake pan or cupcake tin. You may not need all of the mixture depending on the size of your mini cheesecake. (I once formed my own custom 4" mini cake pan out of a disposable aluminum tray.)

3. Whip cream cheese and stir in egg. Pour over crust. You may not need all of the filling depending on the size of your cake.

4. Bake for 10-20 minutes or until top appears set. (Bake time depends on your cake size.)

5. Cool in pan on wire rack for 5 minutes. Use knife to loosen the sides from the tin and allow to cool an additional 5 minutes. Remove from tin carefully, and allow to cool completely. Garnish with raspberries or blueberries if desired. Cover and chill in the refrigerator for at least 1 hour.

FOR ME   *Makes one 9" cheesecake*

1 ½ cups ground graham crackers
1 tablespoon sugar
½ teaspoon ground cinnamon
½ cup butter, melted
3 - 8oz packages of cream cheese, softened
1 cup sugar
1 teaspoon vanilla
3 tablespoons lemon juice
¼ cup milk
3 eggs, slightly beaten
1 cup raspberries (optional)

1. Preheat oven to 375°F.

2. For crust, combine graham crackers, 1 tablespoon sugar, and cinnamon. Stir in melted butter. Press mixture on bottom and sides of 9" springboard pan.

3. To make the filling, beat cream cheese, 1 cup sugar, vanilla, and lemon juice. Beat in milk until smooth. Stir in eggs.

4. Pour filling into pan. Bake 35-40 minutes or until 2 ½" area around outside edge appears set when shaken.

5. Cool in pan on wire rack for 15 minutes. Using a small, sharp knife, loosen crust on sides. Cool for 30 more minutes. Remove sides of pan and allow to cool completely. Garnish with raspberries if desired. Cover and chill for at least 4 hours.

PEANUT BUTTER BACON CHEESECAKE

A savory alternative, the bacon roses are inspired by a story about how Maeby's inability to resist bacon completely backfired on her.

Maeby's been fortunate enough to regularly come to work with me these past few years. Though usually a model citizen, she's had a few slip ups, one of which involved stealing the remainder of my coworker's bacon breakfast. Naturally, I was mortified, so as an apology, I baked him a bouquet of bacon roses complete with an apology card, signed by Maeby of course. Multiple days later, she coincidentally had an "accident" on the same day some of the bacon roses (which sat out) went missing. No one really knows what happened to the roses, but I *think* she likes bacon.

JUST FOR MAEBY

Makes one 5" mini cheesecake

1 cup ground dry dog biscuits
4 tablespoons butter
1 - 8oz package cream cheese
1 egg, beaten
¼ cup all-natural peanut butter
1 strip of bacon

1. Preheat oven to 375°F.

2. Combine ground dog biscuits and butter. Press into ¼ inch layer on the bottom of mini cheesecake pan or cupcake tin.

3. Whip cream cheese and combine with peanut butter and egg. Pour over crust.

4. Bake for 10-20 minutes or until top appears set. (Bake time depends on your cake size.)

5. Cool in pan on wire rack for 5 minutes. Use knife to loosen the sides from the tin and allow to cool an additional 5 minutes. Remove from tin carefully, and allow to cool completely.

6. While the cheesecake cools, preheat the oven to 400°F.

7. Slice your strip of bacon in half in both directions, so you end up with four skinny strips.

8. Roll each strip and secure through all the layers with a toothpick, so that they resemble roses.

9. Bake the miniature bacon roses on a parchment lined baking sheet for 20 minutes. Remove toothpicks when cool.

10. Garnish the cheesecake with miniature bacon roses. Cover and chill in the refrigerator for at least 1 hour.

BAKED ALASKA

For those brave enough, this impressive treat is simply a combination of the Peanut Butter Deep Dish Brownies (pg. 21), Peanut Butter Banana Ice Cream (pg. 71), and some meringue. Though likely a challenge to those who haven't made this before, it can be a really fun adventure in baking.

For those looking to take some short cuts or do a trial run, there are some simple alternatives. Rather than line the entire bowl with cake, you can simply fill the bowl with ice cream and use a layer of cake as a base. Just want to practice your building and meringue skills? Quickly test out this dessert with your human friends by using a boxed cake mix and store bought ice cream.

FOR MAEBY

Serves 4

For the ice cream:
4 frozen, ripe to overripe bananas
¼ cup all-natural peanut butter
Optional: splash of whole milk

For the brownies:
¼ cup honey
3 tablespoons unsalted butter, melted
1 egg white
¼ cup flour
3 tablespoons carob powder
¼ teaspoon baking powder

For the meringue:
2 egg whites (about ¼ cup), room temperature
½ cup honey

1. Make the Ice Cream: Blend bananas and peanut butter in a food processor until smooth.

2. When it starts to look like soft serve, add a splash of whole milk if you'd like a creamier texture.

3. Scoop into freezer safe container and freeze.

4. Make the Brownies: Preheat oven to 350°F.

5. In a medium mixing bowl, beat together honey, butter, and egg white.

6. In a separate bowl, combine flour, carob powder, and baking powder.

7. Stir flour mixture into the liquid mixture until combined.

8. Pour batter into greased or lined 5 inch baking pan. If you do not have a 5 inch baking pan, you can use something else, it may just be a little harder to build the cake.

continued on the next page

9. Bake 20-30 minutes or until toothpick comes out of the center almost clean.

10. Allow the cake to cool completely.

11. Building the Ice Cream Cake: Remove the ice cream from the freezer to allow it to soften. Remove cake from pan and line the sides and bottom of a 4–5 inch plastic lined bowl with cake. You might consider cutting the cake in half horizontally to make two thinner, more flexible cakes. Make sure they are snug and trim any excess cake from the top edge of the bowl.

12. Scoop the softened ice cream into the cake bowl and cover the top with the remaining pieces of cake, sealing it shut and trimming any excess. Cover tightly with plastic wrap and freeze for at least 2 hours.

13. Making the Meringue: Preheat the oven to 400°F. Begin making the meringue once cake & ice cream are frozen. Whisk the egg whites with a stand mixer or hand mixer until you get soft peaks. Slowly add the honey while continuing to mix on high until fully dissolved and you get stiff peaks.

14. Building the Baked Alaska: Remove your ice cream cake from the freezer and remove plastic wrap. Invert onto an ovenproof pie plate or baking dish, with the flat side down. Remove bowl and all plastic wrap.

15. Completely cover the cake in meringue with a spoon or spatula, making sure there are no gaps or holes. Use a spoon or spatula to make swirls or spikes in the meringue by quickly pulling away.

16. Bake about 5 minutes in the oven until meringue starts to lightly brown. Remove from the oven and serve immediately.

FOR ME

Serves 8

For the ice cream:
4 frozen, ripe to overripe bananas
¼ cup all natural peanut butter
Optional: splash of whole milk

For the brownies:
1 ½ cup sugar
¾ cup unsalted butter, melted
3 eggs
1 ½ teaspoon vanilla
¾ cup flour
½ cocoa powder
½ teaspoon baking powder
½ teaspoon salt
6 oz. semi-sweet chocolate chips or peanut butter chips

For the meringue:
6 egg whites (¾ cup), room temperature
1 ½ cup sugar
¼ teaspoon cream of tartar

1. Make the Ice Cream: Blend bananas and peanut butter in a food processor until smooth.

2. When it starts to look like soft serve, add a splash of whole milk if you'd like a creamier texture.

3. Scoop into freezer safe container and freeze.

4. Making the Brownies: Preheat oven to 350°F.

5. In a large mixing bowl, beat together sugar, butter, eggs, and vanilla.

6. In separate bowl, combine flour, cocoa, baking powder, and salt.

7. Stir flour mixture into the butter/sugar mixture until combined.

8. Fold in chocolate chips or peanut butter chips.

9. Pour into a greased 9 inch round cake pan. Bake up to 45 minutes or until toothpick comes out of the center almost clean.

10. Allow cake to cool completely.

11. Building the Ice Cream Cake: Remove the ice cream from the freezer to allow it to soften. Remove cake from pan and line the sides and bottom of an 8 inch plastic lined bowl with cake. You might consider cutting the cake in half horizontally to make two thinner, more flexible cakes. Make sure they are snug and trim any excess cake from the top edge of the bowl.

12. Scoop the softened ice cream into the cake bowl and cover the top with the remaining pieces of cake, sealing it shut and trimming any excess. Cover tightly with plastic wrap and freeze for at least 2 hours.

13. Making the Meringue: Preheat the oven to 400°F. Begin making the meringue once cake & ice cream are frozen. Whisk the egg whites and cream of tartar with a stand mixer or hand mixer on medium high until you get soft peaks. Slowly add the sugar while mixing on high until fully dissolved and you get stiff peaks.

14. Building the Baked Alaska: Remove your ice cream cake from the freezer and remove plastic wrap. Invert onto an ovenproof pie plate or baking dish, with the flat side down. Remove bowl and all plastic wrap.

15. Completely cover the cake in meringue with a spoon or spatula, making sure there are no gaps or holes. Use a spoon or spatula to make swirls or spikes in the meringue by quickly pulling away.

16. Bake about 5 minutes in the oven until meringue starts to lightly brown. Remove from the oven and serve immediately.

INDEX

ABOUT THE AUTHOR

Jen Augello, a Chicago native, resides in New York City with her favorite pup Maeby. From a Sicilian family, some of Jen's earliest memories involve the love of her first dog Jojo and stealing raw cookie dough from her grandmother's kitchen counter. Naturally, that leads to writing a cookbook for dogs.

In addition to regular baking escapades, Jen is a freelance clarinetist and works in production and operations in children's television (*Sesame Street*, *The Not-Too-Late Show with Elmo*, & *Helpsters*) and at classical music organizations such as Lincoln Center and Carnegie Hall. She has long worked to incorporate both local and international audiences into her work, bringing communities together through educational entertainment.

This is Jen's first cookbook, and first publication of any kind. With degrees in chemistry and clarinet performance, Jen finds that baking combines both the precision and transformational fun of chemistry with the creativity and joy of musical performance. Although at times stressful, she has found the experience fun and rewarding, especially as she gets to share so much of it with the book's photogenic star Maeby.

ACKNOWLEDGMENTS

This project was so much fun! A huge thank you to all of the incredible people (and doggies) along the way. It really has meant a lot that so many people have been willing to help, and I never expected such encouragement and support

It goes without saying that this would have never existed without Maeby. I've spent our entire time together trying to think of ways to thank her for how much positivity she's contributed to my life from the moment we met. She inspires confidence, commitment, loyalty, and happiness each and every day, and at the very least, I hope that this book is able to share some of that with the world.

To one of my oldest and best friends Nick Holmes, who was on board before I was even able to finish pitching the idea, thank you for going on this crazy ride with me. Even though we would likely do anything for one another, I definitely owe him for the hundreds of hours, expertise, and challenges over the past 18 months.

To balance our nutty working relationship came Simon Morgan – consultant, editor, production assistant, and now our official tie-breaker. I'm not sure I could have been finished this book without Simon, and I'm so thankful for your support.

A special thank you to the following individuals that helped donate resources, time, and advice:

Erica Gonzalez
Jason Falk
Deborah McMillen
Shane, Jason, and Chris at Hold Fast Kitchen & Spirits (New York City)
The Juilliard School Cafeteria

And, finally, a special thank you to those that helped support this project through our early fundraiser and continuous encouragement:

Charles Augello	Deborah McMillen	Rose Mormino
Linda Carroll	Joseph F. McMillen	Julio Neira
Sarah Lee	Simon Morgan	

Maeby and I look forward to your continued support and look forward to hearing about your baking adventures.

Jen & Maeby

ABOUT THE PHOTOGRAPHER

Nick is a Chicago based graphic designer & pretend music producer with Antlur Creative who has worked on extensive branding, packaging, and websites with national brands & local businesses since 2004.

His passion for photography began at the age of 11 after watching John Acorn on Animal Planet capturing all manner of creatures. Nick did the same, and now, has developed a strange obsession with food photography. (We think he's just always hungry.)

See more of Nick's work at www.antlur.co & www.nickdoesfood.com.